U.S. NATIONAL PARKS
EVERGLADES NATIONAL PARK

by Penelope S. Nelson

pogo

Ideas for Parents and Teachers

Pogo Books let children practice reading informational text while introducing them to nonfiction features such as headings, labels, sidebars, maps, and diagrams, as well as a table of contents, glossary, and index.

Carefully leveled text with a strong photo match offers early fluent readers the support they need to succeed.

Before Reading

- "Walk" through the book and point out the various nonfiction features. Ask the student what purpose each feature serves.
- Look at the glossary together. Read and discuss the words.

Read the Book

- Have the child read the book independently.
- Invite him or her to list questions that arise from reading.

After Reading

- Discuss the child's questions. Talk about how he or she might find answers to those questions.
- Prompt the child to think more. Ask: Everglades National Park is home to many alligators. Why do you think the park makes a good home for this reptile?

Pogo Books are published by Jump!
5357 Penn Avenue South
Minneapolis, MN 55419
www.jumplibrary.com

Library of Congress Cataloging-in-Publication Data

Names: Nelson, Penelope, 1994- author.
Title: Everglades National Park / by Penelope S. Nelson.
Description: Minneapolis, MN: Jump!, Inc., 2020.
Series: U.S. national parks | "Pogo Books."
Includes index.
Identifiers: LCCN 2018051198 (print)
LCCN 2018054543 (ebook)
ISBN 9781641288101 (ebook)
ISBN 9781641288095 (hardcover : alk. paper)
Subjects: LCSH: Everglades National Park (Fla.) Juvenile literature.
Classification: LCC F317.E9 (ebook)
LCC F317.E9 N45 2020 (print)
DDC 975.9/39—dc23
LC record available at https://lccn.loc.gov/2018051198

Editor: Jenna Trnka
Designer: Jenna Casura

Photo Credits: Romrodphoto/Shutterstock, cover; TerryJ/iStock, 1, 14; topten22photo/Shutterstock, 3; Robert La Rosa/Shutterstock, 4; f11photo/Shutterstock, 5; YinYang/iStock, 6-7; Joe Pearl Photography/iStock, 8-9tl; jo Crebbin/Shutterstock, 8-9tr; 33karen33/ iStock, 8-9bl; Agami Photo Agency/Shutterstock, 8-9br; Ovidiu Hrubaru/Shutterstock, 10; Tom Salyer/ Alamy, 11; Dennis K. Johnson/Getty, 12-13; Golden Pixels LLC/Shutterstock, 15; National Geographic Image Collection/Alamy, 16-17; SanderMeertinsPhotography/ Shutterstock, 18-19tl; imageBROKER/Alamy, 18-19tr; Brian Lasenby/Shutterstock, 18-19bl; FloridaStock/ Shutterstock, 18-19br; AlpamayoPhoto/iStock, 20-21; Eric Isselee/Shutterstock, 23.

Printed in the United States of America at Corporate Graphics in North Mankato, Minnesota.

TABLE OF CONTENTS

CHAPTER 1

HOT AND HUMID

Would you like to see Florida's marsh birds? See alligators! They can grow up to 15 feet (4.6 meters) long!

See them from an airboat! You can do this at Everglades National Park. Most of the park is made up of marshy **coastland**.

airboat

mangrove
forest

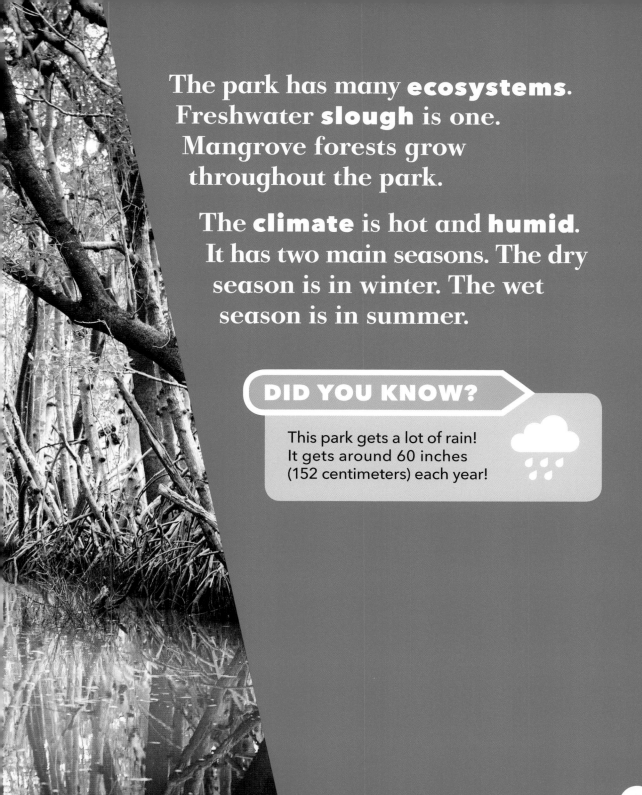

The park has many **ecosystems**. Freshwater **slough** is one. Mangrove forests grow throughout the park.

The **climate** is hot and **humid**. It has two main seasons. The dry season is in winter. The wet season is in summer.

DID YOU KNOW?

This park gets a lot of rain! It gets around 60 inches (152 centimeters) each year!

The park was founded in 1947. People fought to **conserve** this special area. Why? It is home to many special plants and animals!

Many **endangered species** are here. American alligators, Florida panthers, West Indian manatees, and wood storks all make their homes in the park.

WHAT DO YOU THINK?

National parks are owned by the U.S. government. They protect special places in nature. Why? So people can visit them. The plants and animals that live here are protected, too! Why do you think this is important?

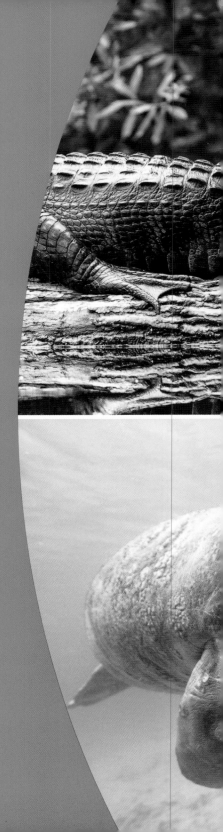

alligator

panther

manatee

wood stork

CHAPTER 2

PEOPLE AND THE PARK

Humans have a long history here. A **missile** base sits in the middle of the park. No missiles were launched here. But you can take a tour and see where they were kept!

missile

Some human impacts are harmful. **Climate change** causes rising water levels in the park. It also worsens **hurricanes**. The park is on the coast. This means it is in the path of many hurricanes. They can cause a lot of damage.

hurricane damage

park ranger

People work hard to care for the park. They repair hurricane damage. They study the park. They help keep it clean. They care for the animals here. Park rangers teach visitors how to help!

WHAT DO YOU THINK?

Park rangers teach visitors how to help care for the park and its wildlife. Would you like to do this? Why or why not?

CHAPTER 3

EXPLORE THE PARK

Explore the park by airboat, canoe, or kayak! The Wilderness Waterway goes through the park. A guide can help you **navigate** the waters.

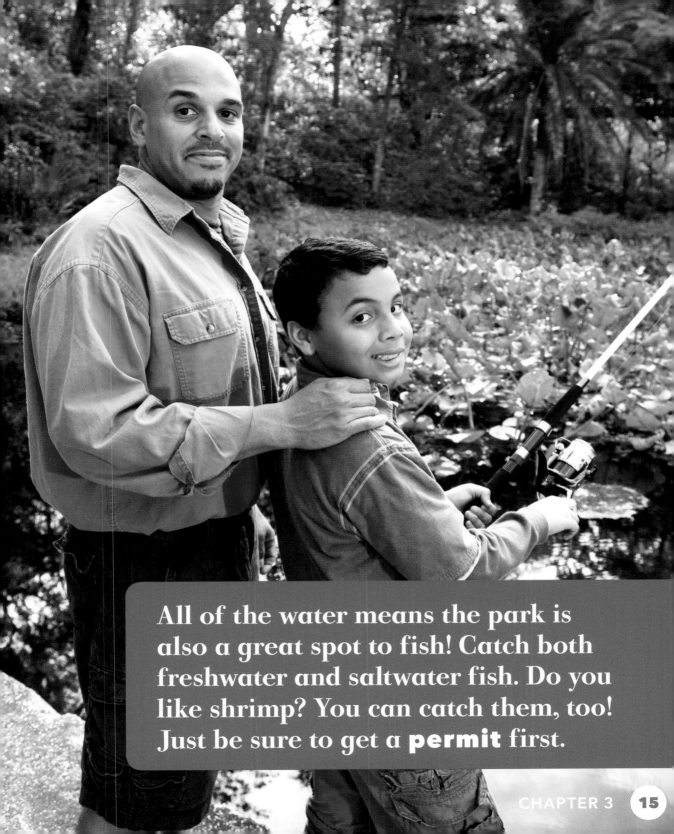

All of the water means the park is also a great spot to fish! Catch both freshwater and saltwater fish. Do you like shrimp? You can catch them, too! Just be sure to get a **permit** first.

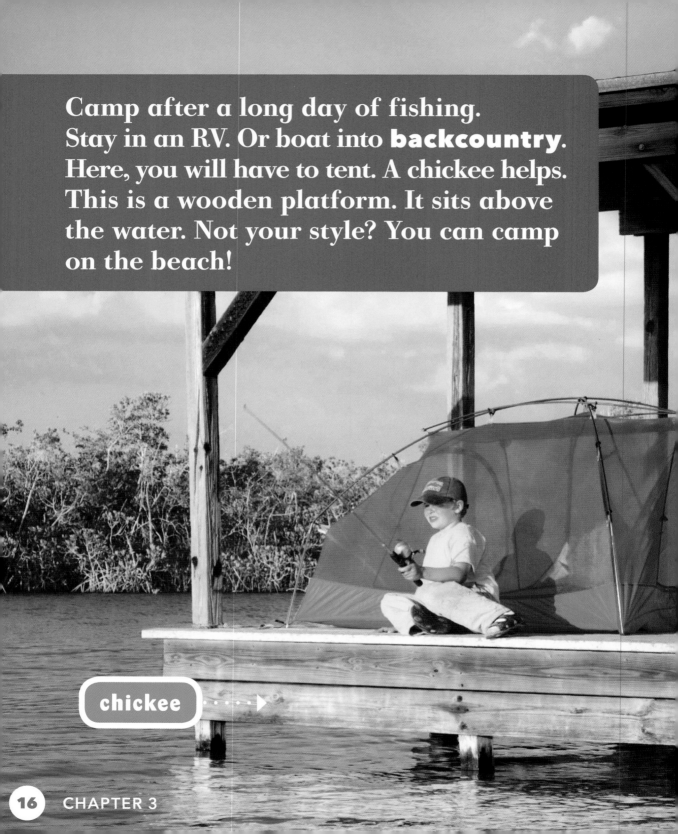

Camp after a long day of fishing. Stay in an RV. Or boat into **backcountry**. Here, you will have to tent. A chickee helps. This is a wooden platform. It sits above the water. Not your style? You can camp on the beach!

chickee ·····▶

Camping here is fun. But it can be hard work! There are many mosquitoes and flies. It can be very hot, sunny, and humid. Be prepared. Here are some of the things you may need to boat and camp in the Everglades.

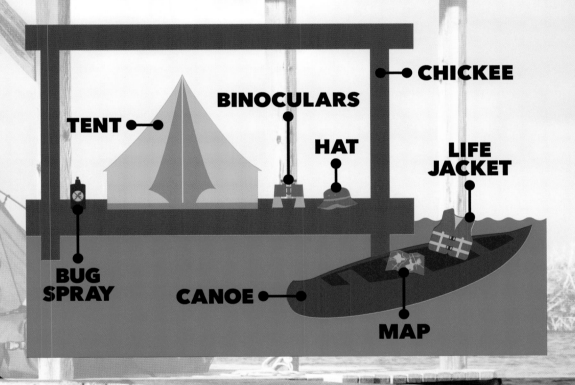

CHICKEE

TENT

BINOCULARS

HAT

LIFE JACKET

BUG SPRAY

CANOE

MAP

You will likely see marsh birds on your visit. Many birds make their homes here. How many? More than 360 kinds! These four kinds of birds wade in the warm, shallow water. Why? Their food is in the water! Some birds rest here during **migrations**.

heron

ibis

spoonbill

purple gallinule

observation tower

Do you like being active?
Check out the park's many trails.
Hike the Coastal Prairie Trail.
Bike the Shark Valley Loop.
At the end, climb to the top
of an observation tower.
Look out over the park!

Everglades National Park is
full of wonders! What would
you like to see?

QUICK FACTS & TOOLS

EVERGLADES NATIONAL PARK

Location: Florida

Year Established: 1947

Area: 1,542,526 acres
(624,238 hectares)

Approximate Yearly Visitors:
1 million

Top Attractions:
Anhinga Trail, Wilderness
Waterway, Shark Valley
Observation Tower,
airboat tours

Number of Campground Sites:
387

GLOSSARY

backcountry: Underdeveloped, rural areas.

climate: The weather typical of a place over a long period of time.

climate change: Global warming and other changes in the weather and weather patterns that are happening because of human activity.

coastland: Land that borders the sea.

conserve: To save something, such as animals, wildlife, and land, from loss.

ecosystems: Areas that include all of the living and nonliving things within them.

endangered species: Plants or animals that are in danger of becoming extinct.

humid: Moist and warm weather.

hurricanes: Violent storms with heavy rain and high winds.

migrations: The movements of animals from one area or climate to another at particular times of the year.

missile: A weapon that is aimed at a target.

navigate: To find where you are and where you need to go when traveling.

permit: An official document that gives someone permission to do something.

slough: A swampy area of land.

INDEX

TO LEARN MORE

Finding more information is as easy as 1, 2, 3.

① **Go to www.factsurfer.com**

② **Enter "EvergladesNationalPark" into the search box.**

③ **Choose your book to see a list of websites.**

FACT SURFER